To My Uncle, I Want to Hear Your Story

A Guided Journal to Share His Life & His Love

Jeffrey Mason

Hear Your Story Books

"Everything
I am,
you helped
me to be."
— Author Unknown

This Book Holds & Shares The Life Stories of:

_____

_____

"An uncle is
a teacher,
a mentor
a friend
for all
of our lives."
– Author Unknown

About This Book

"The thing that interests me most about family history is the gap between the things we think we know about our families and the realities." – Jeremy Hardy

Our families are our connections to what came before and what comes after. They show us the magnificence of what can happen when we set aside our own needs, ignore our differences, and allow ourselves to join with others.

Our connections with each other are strengthened when we hear and understand each other's life stories, and "To My Uncle, I Want to Hear Your Story" provides a place for some of the best storytellers of all to share their lives and their experiences.

Uncles play a special role in our lives. They are the one who we could ask anything, they are the one who would help us without hesitation, the one who always made things fun. He encouraged us to dream big dreams and to believe in all you could be.

"To My Uncle, I Want to Hear Your Story" is the perfect way for them to share your life, your adventures.

Dedicated to the timeless and sacred art of passing on, sharing, and learning from the collective stories of our families.

THE DAY YOU WERE BORN

"Uncle: Someone who helps, advises, and encourages; great at telling funny family stories." — Author Unknown

What is your birthdate?
_____

What was your full name at birth?
_____

Were you named after a relative or someone else of significance?
_____
_____
_____

In what city were you born?
_____

What was your length and weight at birth?
_____

Were you born in a hospital? If not, where?
_____
_____

What were your first words?
_____
_____

To My Uncle, I Want to Hear Your Story

THE DAY YOU WERE BORN

"The great use of life is to spend it for something that will outlast it." — William James

How old were you when you started to walk?

_____

How old were your parents when you were born?

_____

_____

How did your parents describe you as a baby?

_____

_____

_____

_____

_____

_____

_____

_____

THE DAY YOU WERE BORN

"You can tell your uncle stuff that you could not tell your dad."
— Dusty Baker

What stories have you been told about the day you were born?

_____
_____
_____
_____
_____
_____
_____
_____
_____
_____
_____
_____
_____
_____

To My Uncle, I Want to Hear Your Story

THE DAY YOU WERE BORN
"Creativity is intelligence having fun."
— Albert Einstein

What is a favorite childhood memory?

_____
_____
_____
_____
_____
_____
_____
_____
_____
_____
_____
_____
_____
_____
_____

WHAT HAPPENED THE YEAR YOU WERE BORN?

"A family doesn't have to perfect; it just needs to be united."
— Author Unknown

Google the following for the year you were born:
What are some notable events that occurred?

_____

_____

_____

_____

What movie won the Academy Award for Best Picture? Who won for Best Actor and Best Actress?

_____

_____

_____

What were a few popular movies that came out that year?

_____

_____

_____

_____

_____

To My Uncle, I Want to Hear Your Story

WHAT HAPPENED THE YEAR YOU WERE BORN?

"Growing old is mandatory. Growing up is optional."
— Walt Disney

What song was on the top of the Billboard charts?

_____

Who was the leader of the country (President, Prime Minister, etc.)?

_____

What were a few popular television shows?

_____

_____

_____

_____

_____

What were the prices for the following items?
- A loaf of bread:
- A gallon of milk:
- A cup of coffee:
- A dozen eggs:
- The average cost of a new home:
- A first-class stamp:
- A new car:
- A gallon of gas:
- A movie ticket:

GROWING UP

"An amazing uncle is like a glass of refreshing lemonade in the hot summer of life." — Author Unknown

How would you describe yourself when you were a kid?

_____
_____
_____
_____

Did you have a nickname when you were growing up? If yes, how did you get it?

_____

Who were your best friends in your elementary school days? Are you still in contact with them?

_____
_____
_____
_____

What were your regular chores? Did you get an allowance? How much was it and what did you spend it on?

_____
_____
_____

GROWING UP

"You don't stop laughing when you grow old, you grow old when you stop laughing." — George Bernard Shaw

Describe what your room looked like when you were growing up. Was it messy or clean? Did you have paintings or posters on the walls? What were the main colors?

_____
_____
_____
_____
_____
_____
_____
_____
_____

What is one thing you miss about being a kid?

_____
_____
_____

GROWING UP

"Friends come and go, but relatives tend to accumulate."
— Author Unknown

Did you have braces when you were a kid?

_____

What is your favorite book from your childhood or teen years?

_____

_____

_____

What was a typical Saturday like when you were a kid? What did you spend the day doing?

_____

_____

_____

_____

_____

_____

_____

GROWING UP

"Not how long, but how well you have lived is the main thing."
— Seneca

What is a favorite childhood memory?

___

TRIVIA

"Do not go where the path may lead, go instead where there is no path and leave a trail." — Ralph Waldo Emerson

What is your favorite flavor of ice cream?

_____

How do you like your coffee?

_____

_____

If you could live anywhere in the world for a year with all expenses paid, where would you choose?

_____

_____

_____

How do you like your eggs cooked?

_____

Preference: cook or clean?

_____

What is your shoe size?

_____

What superpower would you choose for yourself?

_____

_____

TRIVIA

"There can be no keener revelation of a society's soul
than the way in which it treats its children." — Nelson Mandela

Do you have any allergies?

_____

_____

_____

What is your biggest fear?

_____

_____

What would you order as your last meal?

_____

_____

_____

_____

Have you ever broken a bone? Which one(s) and how?

_____

_____

What is your favorite sandwich?

_____

THE TEENAGE YEARS

"It takes courage to grow up and become who you really are."
— e.e. cummings

How would you describe yourself when you were a teenager?

_____
_____
_____
_____

How did you dress and style your hair during your teens?

_____
_____
_____
_____
_____
_____

Did you hang out with a group or just a few close friends? Are you still close with any of them?

_____
_____
_____
_____

To My Uncle, I Want to Hear Your Story

THE TEENAGE YEARS
"Raising teenagers is like nailing jell-o to a tree."
— Author Unknown

Describe a typical Friday or Saturday night during your high school years.

_____

_____

_____

_____

Did you have a curfew?

_____

Did you date during your high school years?

_____

_____

Did you go to any school dances? What were they like?

_____

_____

_____

_____

Who taught you to drive and in what kind of car?

_____

_____

THE TEENAGE YEARS

"Each of us is tomorrow's ancestors."
— Author Unknown

How old were you when you got your first car? What kind of car was it (year, make, and model)?

_____

_____

What school activities or sports did you participate in?

_____

_____

_____

_____

_____

What did you like and dislike about high school?

_____

_____

_____

_____

_____

THE TEENAGE YEARS

"Keep true to the dreams of your youth."
— Friedrich Schiller

What were your grades like?

_____

_____

Did you have a favorite subject and a least favorite?

_____

_____

_____

What are a few favorite songs from your high school years?

_____

_____

_____

_____

_____

_____

_____

THE TEENAGE YEARS

"Be yourself; everyone else is already taken."
— Oscar Wilde

Knowing all you know now, what advice would you give to your teenage self? What might you have done differently in school if you knew then what you know now?

_____

_____

_____

_____

_____

_____

_____

_____

_____

_____

_____

_____

_____

THE TEENAGE YEARS

"Little children, headache; big children, heartache."
— Italian Proverb

Write about a teacher, coach, or other mentor who had a significant impact on you when you were growing up.

THE TEENAGE YEARS

"The best substitute for experience is being a teenager."
— Author Unknown

Write about a favorite memory from your teenage years.

___

WHERE HAVE YOU LIVED?
"Home is where our story begins."
— Author Unknown

List the cities where you have lived during your lifetime. Include the dates if you can remember them?

BEGINNINGS

"We don't stop going to school when we graduate."
— Carol Burnett

What did you do after high school? Did you get a job, serve in the military, go to college or a trade school? Something else?

_____
_____
_____
_____

What led you to make this choice?

_____
_____
_____
_____
_____
_____

If you went to college or trade school, what was your major/the focus of your education?

_____
_____
_____

BEGINNINGS

"Funcle: like a Dad, only cooler."
— Author Unknown

How did this time period impact who you are today?

If you could go back, what, if anything, would you change about this period of your life? Why?

WORK & CAREER

"Even if you're on the right track, you'll get run over if you just sit there." — Will Rogers

When you were a kid, what did you want to be when you grew up?

_____

_____

What was your first job? How old were you? How much were you paid?

_____

_____

How many jobs have you had during your lifetime? List a few of your favorites.

_____

_____

_____

_____

What is the least favorite job you have had?

_____

_____

_____

WORK & CAREER

"I'm a great believer in luck, and I find the harder I work, the more I have of it." — Thomas Jefferson

Is there a job or profession your parents wanted you to pursue? What was it?

_____

_____

_____

When people ask you what profession you are/were in, your response is...

_____

_____

_____

How did you get into this career?

_____

_____

_____

_____

_____

WORK & CAREER

"Choose a job you love and you will never have to work a day in your life." — Confucius

What are/were the best parts of this profession?

_____
_____
_____
_____
_____
_____
_____

What aspects did you or do you dislike about it?

_____
_____
_____
_____
_____
_____

WORK & CAREER

"If people knew how hard I worked to get my mastery, it wouldn't seem so wonderful after all." — Michelangelo

Who was the best boss you ever had? Why were they such a good manager?

_____
_____
_____
_____
_____
_____

What are some of your work and career-related achievements that you are proudest of?

_____
_____
_____
_____
_____
_____
_____

TRIVIA

"Where we love is home - home that our feet may leave, but not our hearts." — Oliver Wendell Holmes, Sr

Have you ever been told that you look like someone famous? If yes, who?

_____

_____

_____

What is your morning routine?

_____

_____

_____

_____

_____

What is a favorite guilty pleasure?

_____

_____

_____

Which television family most reminds you of your family?

_____

_____

TRIVIA

"The only rock I know that stays steady, the only institution I know that works, is the family." — Lee Iacocca

Did you have braces? If yes, how old were you when you got them?

_____

Do you like roller coasters?

_____

_____

What name would you choose if you had to change your first name?

_____

Did you ever skip school?

_____

If yes, did you get away with it and what did you do during the time you should have been in class?

_____

_____

_____

_____

_____

To My Uncle, I Want to Hear Your Story

YOUR FAMILY TREE

"Families are like branches on a tree. We grow in different directions, yet our roots remain as one." — Author Unknown

_____
My Great-Grandmother
(My Grandmother's Mom)

_____
My Great-Grandmother
(My Grandfather's Mom)

_____
My Great-Grandfather
(My Grandmother's Dad)

_____
My Great-Grandfather
(My Grandfather's Dad)

_____
My Grandmother
(My Mom's Mom)

_____
My Grandfather
(My Mom's Dad)

_____
My Mother

To My Uncle, I Want to Hear Your Story

YOUR FAMILY TREE

"To forget one's ancestors is to be a brook without a source, a tree without a root." — Chinese Proverb

My Great-Grandmother
(My Grandmother's Mom)

My Great-Grandmother
(My Grandfather's Mom)

My Great-Grandfather
(My Grandmother's Dad)

My Great-Grandfather
(My Grandfather's Dad)

My Grandmother
(My Dad's Mom)

My Grandfather
(My Dad's Dad)

My Father

PARENTS & GRANDPARENTS

"He who has no fools, knaves, or beggars in his family was begot by a flash of lightning." — Old English Proverb

Where was your mother born and where did she grow up?

How would you describe her?

In what ways are you most like your mother?

PARENTS & GRANDPARENTS

"Appreciate your parents. You never know what sacrifices they went through for you." — Unknown

Where was your father born and where did he grow up?

_____
_____
_____

How would you describe him?

_____
_____
_____

In what ways are you most like your father?

_____
_____
_____
_____
_____
_____
_____

PARENTS & GRANDPARENTS

"It is a desirable thing to be well-descended,
but the glory belongs to our ancestors." — Plutarch

What is a favorite memory of your mother?

_____
_____
_____
_____
_____
_____
_____
_____
_____
_____
_____
_____
_____

PARENTS & GRANDPARENTS

"Why waste your money looking up your family tree? Just go into politics and your opponents will do it for you." — Mark Twain

What is a favorite memory of your father?

PARENTS & GRANDPARENTS

"Love is the chain whereby to bind a child to its parents."
— Abraham Lincoln

What was your mother's maiden name?

_____

Do you know from what part(s) of the world your mother's family originates?

_____

_____

_____

Do you know your father's mother's maiden name?

_____

_____

Do you know from what part(s) of the world your father's family originates?

_____

_____

_____

How did your parents meet?

_____

_____

_____

PARENTS & GRANDPARENTS
"Next to God, thy parents."
— William Penn

How would you describe their relationship?

___

What were your parents' occupations?

___

Did either of them have any unique talents or skills?

___

Did either of them serve in the military?

PARENTS & GRANDPARENTS

"When a society or a civilization perishes, one condition can always be found. They forgot where they came from." — Carle Sandburg

What is a favorite family tradition that was passed down from your parents or grandparents?

_____

_____

_____

What are a few of your favorite things that your mother or father would cook for the family?

_____

_____

_____

_____

What were your grandparents like on your mother's side?

_____

_____

_____

_____

_____

PARENTS & GRANDPARENTS

"A father's goodness is higher than the mountain,
a mother's goodness deeper than the sea." — Japanese Proverb

Do you know where your mother's parents were born and grew up?

_____

_____

_____

_____

What were your grandparents like on your father's side?

_____

_____

_____

_____

_____

Do you know where your father's parents were born and grew up?

_____

_____

_____

PARENTS & GRANDPARENTS

"There is no school equal to a decent home and no teacher equal to a virtuous parent." — Mahatma Gandhi

What is some of the best advice your mother gave you?

_____

_____

_____

_____

_____

_____

_____

_____

_____

_____

_____

_____

_____

_____

PARENTS & GRANDPARENTS

"If you cannot get rid of the family skeleton, you may as well make it dance." — George Bernard Shaw

What is some of the best advice your father gave you?

PARENTS & GRANDPARENTS

"When an elder dies, it is as if an entire library has burned to the ground." — African Proverb

Did you ever meet your great-grandparents on either side of your family? If yes, what were they like?

_____

_____

_____

_____

_____

_____

_____

_____

_____

_____

_____

_____

_____

PARENTS & GRANDPARENTS

"What greater thing is there for human souls than to feel that they are joined for life." — George Eliot

What other individuals had a major role in helping you grow up?

_____
_____
_____
_____
_____
_____
_____
_____
_____
_____
_____
_____
_____
_____
_____

YOUR SIBLINGS

"Brothers and sisters are as close as hands and feet."
— Vietnamese Saying

How many siblings do you have?

_____

Are you the oldest, middle, or youngest?

_____

List your siblings' names in order of their ages. Make sure to include yourself.

_____

_____

_____

_____

Which of your siblings were you the closest with growing up?

_____

_____

Which of your siblings are you the closest with in your adult years?

_____

_____

YOUR SIBLINGS

"The greatest gift our parents ever gave us was each other."
— Author Unknown

How would you describe each of your siblings when they were kids?

_____
_____
_____
_____
_____
_____
_____

How would you describe each of your siblings as adults?

_____
_____
_____
_____
_____
_____
_____

YOUR SIBLINGS
"First a brother, then a bother, now a friend."
— Author Unknown

In the following pages, share some favorite memories of each of your siblings. If you're an only child, feel free to share memories of close friends or cousins.

YOUR SIBLINGS

"What causes sibling rivalry? Having more than one kid."
— Tim Allen

Memories...

YOUR SIBLINGS

"Siblings know how to push each other's buttons, but they also know how to mend things faster than anyone." — Author Unknown

Memories...

_____

_____

_____

_____

_____

_____

_____

_____

_____

_____

_____

_____

_____

_____

YOUR SIBLINGS

"The advantage of growing up with siblings is that you become very good at fractions." — Author Unknown

Memories...

TRIVIA

"Those who have no knowledge of what has gone before them must forever remain children." — Cicero

If you could do any one thing for a day, what would it be?

_____

_____

_____

What do you listen to when you are alone in the car?

_____

_____

How old were you when you got your first traffic ticket? What was it for?

_____

_____

_____

Pick one that best describes you:
- ☐ I am very handy around the house.
- ☐ I can fix a few things.
- ☐ It is in everyone's best interest that I hire someone.

Do you or have you ever played a musical instrument? Which one(s)?

_____

_____

TRIVIA

"Respect your ancestors for you are the
result of a thousand loves." — Unknown

What is your definition of success?

_____

_____

_____

What do you do better than anyone else in the family?

_____

_____

_____

If you could only eat three things for the next year (with no effect on your health), what would you pick?

_____

_____

_____

What is a favorite memory from the last twelve months?

_____

_____

_____

_____

MORE ABOUT ME

"To find yourself, think for yourself."
— Socrates

What would you title your autobiography?

___

What is your favorite quote?

___

What are the main values you have tried to live your life by?

___

MORE ABOUT ME

"The only journey is the journey within."
— Rainer Maria Rilke

What life experiences would you say have had the largest impact on who you are today?

_____
_____
_____
_____
_____
_____
_____
_____
_____
_____
_____
_____
_____

MORE ABOUT ME

"Those who wish to sing, always find a song."
— Swedish Proverb

Who are the people who have had the largest impact on you becoming who you are today?

_____
_____
_____
_____
_____
_____
_____
_____
_____
_____
_____
_____
_____
_____

MORE ABOUT ME

"The best way to predict your future is to create it."
— Abraham Lincoln

What are a few of your proudest personal accomplishments?

___
___
___
___
___
___
___
___
___
___
___
___
___
___
___

MORE ABOUT ME

"The more you know yourself, the more patience you have for what you see in others." — Erik Erikson

What is the hardest thing you have had to overcome in your life?

_____
_____
_____
_____
_____
_____
_____
_____
_____
_____
_____
_____
_____

MORE ABOUT ME

"If the only prayer you ever say in your entire
life is thank you, it will be enough." — Meister Eckhart

Write about the decisions, actions, and people that helped you succeed in overcoming this challenging time.

SPIRITUALITY & RELIGION

"For we walk by faith, not by sight."
— 2 Corinthians 5, King James Version

What do you believe is the purpose of life?

_____
_____
_____
_____
_____
_____
_____
_____

Which has the most impact on our lives: fate or free will?

_____
_____
_____
_____

SPIRITUALITY & RELIGION

"If you lose faith, you lose all."
— Eleanor Roosevelt

Were your parents religious when you were growing up? If yes, how did they express their spiritual beliefs?

_____
_____
_____
_____
_____
_____
_____
_____
_____
_____
_____
_____

SPIRITUALITY & RELIGION

"The smallest seed of faith is better than the largest fruit of happiness." — Henry David Thoreau

If you are religious or spiritual, how have your beliefs and practices changed over the course of your life?

SPIRITUALITY & RELIGION

"Faith is a living, daring confidence in God's grace, so sure and certain that a man could stake his life on it a thousand times." — Martin Luther

What religious or spiritual practices do you incorporate into your daily life today, if any?

Do you believe in miracles? Have you experienced one?

To My Uncle, I Want to Hear Your Story

LOVE & ROMANCE
"If I know what love is, it is because of you!"
— Hermann Hesse

Do you believe in love at first sight?

_____

_____

_____

Do you believe in soulmates?

_____

_____

_____

How old were you when you had your first kiss?

_____

What age were you when you went on your first date?

_____

Can you remember who it was with and what you did?

_____

_____

_____

_____

LOVE & ROMANCE

"Love must be as much a light as it is a flame."
— Henry David Thoreau

How old were you when you had your first steady relationship? Who was it with?

_____

How many times in your life have you been in love?

_____

_____

What are some of the most important qualities of a successful relationship?

_____

_____

_____

_____

_____

_____

_____

_____

LOVE & ROMANCE

"Attention is the rarest and purest form of generosity."
— Simone Weil

Did you have any celebrity crushes when you were young?

_____

_____

_____

_____

Were you ever in a relationship with someone your parents did not approve of?

_____

_____

_____

Have you ever written someone or had someone write you a love poem or song?

_____

If yes, write a few lines that you may remember.

_____

_____

_____

_____

_____

LOVE & ROMANCE

"I wish I had done everything on Earth with you."
— F. Scott Fitzgerald, *The Great Gatsby*

In what ways do you feel your parents' relationship influenced how you have approached love and marriage?

_____

_____

_____

_____

_____

_____

Write about a favorite romantic moment.

_____

_____

_____

_____

_____

_____

_____

LOVE & ROMANCE

"Love loves to love love."
— James Joyce

How did you meet your spouse/partner?

What was your first impression of them?

What is your proposal story?

LOVE & ROMANCE

"We loved with a love that was more than love."
— Edgar Allan Poe, *Annabel Lee*

What was your wedding like? Where was it held and who was there? Any good wedding day stories?

TRAVEL

"Once a year, go someplace you've never been before."
— Dali Lama

Do you have a valid passport?
_____

How do you feel about cruises?
_____
_____

How do you feel about flying?
_____

What are a few of your favorite places that you've traveled to?
_____
_____
_____
_____
_____
_____
_____

TRAVEL
"Life is short, and the world is wide."
— Author Unknown

What is a favorite travel memory?

TRAVEL BUCKET LIST

"Man cannot discover new oceans unless he has the courage to lose sight of the shore." — André Gide

List the top 10 places you would visit if money and time were no concern.

1. _____

_____

2. _____

_____

3. _____

_____

4. _____

_____

5. _____

_____

TRAVEL BUCKET LIST

"The world is a book, and those who do not travel read only one page." — Saint Augustine

6. _____

7. _____

8. _____

9. _____

10. _____

LIFE MILESTONE MOMENTS

"When people throw stones at you, convert them into milestones."
— Author Unknown

Milestone Moments

When we look at our own life course, we will see times when our path has been smooth and unheeded and other stretches when it has been winding and uphill with stops and starts along the way.

We will also discover instances when our life path suddenly became harder – or easier – or went in a completely different direction.

These are those milestone moments, marks of time when we made a key decision, when something transformative happened to us, or when a goal we were working for was finally achieved.

Keeping these milestone moments fresh in our minds allows us to learn, to grow, to give thanks, and to celebrate. This awareness makes us stronger and more understanding of the fact that one single day can change everything.

Remembering and knowing that a single choice or a single day can change everything helps us cherish all the days of our lives. We become more willing to make hard choices and take positive risks.

We become brave in our goals, and we work harder to achieve them. We see more of our self-value, and we make ourselves and our ambitions a priority.

To My Uncle, I Want to Hear Your Story

LIFE MILESTONE MOMENTS
"A milestone is less date and more definition."
— Rands

A milestone moment I can identify in my life is...

_____

_____

_____

What were the circumstances that led up to this moment?

_____

_____

_____

What were the changes to you and your life that came from this milestone moment?

_____

_____

_____

_____

_____

_____

_____

LIFE MILESTONE MOMENTS

"Remember to celebrate milestones as you
prepare for the road ahead." — Nelson Mandela

What is a second milestone moment from your life that you can think of?

_____

_____

_____

What were the circumstances that led up to this moment?

_____

_____

_____

What were the changes to you and your life that came from this milestone moment?

_____

_____

_____

_____

_____

_____

LIFE MILESTONE MOMENTS

"Sometimes the hardest thing and the right thing are the same thing." — Author Unknown

What is a third milestone moment from your life that you can think of?

_____

_____

_____

What were the circumstances that led up to this moment?

_____

_____

_____

What were the changes to you and your life that came from this milestone moment?

_____

_____

_____

_____

_____

_____

_____

POLITICAL STUFF

"Each person must live their life as a model for others."
— Rosa Parks

Which best describes how you feel about having political discussions:
- ☐ I would rather not.
- ☐ I prefer to have them with people whose views match mine.
- ☐ I love a good debate.

How old were you the first time you voted?

_____

What are the biggest differences in your political views today and when you were in your early twenties?

_____

_____

_____

_____

Have you ever taken part in a march or boycott? What issues, if any, could motivate you to join one?

_____

_____

_____

_____

POLITICAL STUFF

"In politics stupidity is not a handicap."
— Napoleon Bonaparte

When was the last time you voted?

_____

In what ways do you agree and disagree with the political choices of younger generations?

_____

_____

_____

_____

_____

_____

If you woke up to find yourself in charge of the country, what are the first three things you would enact or change?

One: _____

_____

Two: _____

_____

Three: _____

_____

SPORTS MEMORIES

"Anyone can be a father, but it takes
someone special to be a dad." — Wade Boggs

When you were a kid, did you ever think about being a professional athlete? In which sports?

_____

_____

Growing up, what was your favorite sport? Did you have a favorite team?

_____

_____

_____

_____

Who is your favorite player of all time in any sport?

_____

_____

_____

If money and time were no object, what sporting event would you most want to attend?

_____

_____

_____

SPORTS MEMORIES

"My father gave me the greatest gift anyone could
give another person, he believed in me." — Jim Valvano

What was the first professional sporting event you attended in person?

_____

_____

_____

What was the most crushing defeat you experienced playing or watching a sporting event?

_____

_____

_____

Is there a sporting event you saw as a kid that you still vividly remember?

_____

_____

_____

What is your favorite sports movie?

_____

_____

_____

MOVIES, MUSIC, TELEVISION, & BOOKS

"Every traveler has a home of his own, and he learns to appreciate it the more from his wandering." — Charles Dickens

What movie have you watched the greatest number of times?

_____

_____

What movie or television show can you remember loving when you were a kid?

_____

_____

Who would you cast to play yourself in the movie of your life? How about for the rest of your family?

_____

_____

_____

_____

_____

_____

_____

_____

MOVIES, MUSIC, TELEVISION, & BOOKS

"Little souls find their way to you whether they're from your womb or someone else's." — Sheryl Crow

What are your favorite genres of music?

_____

_____

_____

_____

Which decades had the best music?

_____

_____

_____

_____

What is the first record (or cassette, cd, etc.) you can remember buying or being given as a gift?

_____

_____

What song do you like today that would make your younger self cringe?

_____

_____

MOVIES, MUSIC, TELEVISION, & BOOKS

"The way I see it, if you want the rainbow, you gotta put up with the rain." — Dolly Parton

What is a song from your teens that reminds you of a special event or moment?

_____

_____

_____

What song would you pick as the theme song of your life?

_____

_____

_____

What was the first concert you attended? Where was it held and when?

_____

_____

_____

How has your taste in music changed over the years?

_____

_____

_____

_____

MOVIES, MUSIC, TELEVISION, & BOOKS

"Life is a flower of which love is the honey."
— Victor Hugo

What television show from the past do you wish was still on the air?

_____

If you could be cast in any television show or movie, past or present, which one would you choose?

_____

What are some favorite books from your childhood and/or teenage years?

_____

_____

_____

What book or books have majorly impacted the way you think, work, or live your life?

_____

_____

_____

_____

_____

TOP TEN MOVIES

"Adults are just outdated children."
— Dr. Seuss

List up to ten of your most favorite movies:

1. _____

2. _____

3. _____

4. _____

5. _____

6. _____

7. _____

8. _____

9. _____

10. _____

To My Uncle, I Want to Hear Your Story

TOP TEN SONGS
"The music is not in the notes, but in the silence in between."
— Wolfgang Amadeus Mozart

List up to ten of your most favorite songs:

1. _____

2. _____

3. _____

4. _____

5. _____

6. _____

7. _____

8. _____

9. _____

10. _____

TOP TEN TELEVISION SHOWS

"Television is simply automated day-dreaming."
— Lee Lovinger

List up to ten of your most favorite television shows:

1. _____

2. _____

3. _____

4. _____

5. _____

6. _____

7. _____

8. _____

9. _____

10. _____

TOP TEN BOOKS

"A room without books is like a body without a soul."
— Cicero

List up to ten of your most favorite books:

1. _____

2. _____

3. _____

4. _____

5. _____

6. _____

7. _____

8. _____

9. _____

10. _____

TRIVIA

"The way I see it, if you want the rainbow,
you gotta put up with the rain." — Dolly Parton

If you could travel through time and had to choose, who would you meet: your ancestors or your descendants? Why?

_____

_____

_____

What are five things you are grateful for?

_____

_____

_____

_____

Who would you invite if you could have dinner with any five people who have ever lived?

_____

_____

_____

_____

TRIVIA

"Life is a succession of lessons which must be lived to be understood." — Helen Keller

If you were forced to sing karaoke, what song would you perform?

_____

_____

What is your favorite holiday and why?

_____

_____

_____

_____

Which ten-year period of your life has been your favorite so far and why?

_____

_____

_____

_____

_____

ROOM FOR MORE

"A tree's strength is found in its roots; its gifts, in its branches."
— Author Unknown

The following pages are for you to expand on some of your answers, to share more memories, and/or to write notes to your loved ones:

ROOM FOR MORE

"Be less curious about people and more curious about ideas."
— Marie Curie

ROOM FOR MORE

"A moment lasts for seconds but the memory of it lasts forever."
— Author Unknown

To My Uncle, I Want to Hear Your Story

ROOM FOR MORE
"A happy family is but an earlier heaven."
— George Bernard Shaw

To My Uncle, I Want to Hear Your Story

ROOM FOR MORE
"Compassion is the chief law of human existence."
— Fyodor Dostoyevsky

ROOM FOR MORE

"The most important thing in the world is family and love."
— John Wooden

ROOM FOR MORE

"Obstacles are those things you see when you take your eyes off the goal." — Henry Ford

ROOM FOR MORE

"Having somewhere to go is home. Having someone to love is family. Having both is a blessing." — Author Unknown

ROOM FOR MORE

"Doing nothing for others is the undoing of ourselves."
— Horace Mann

ROOM FOR MORE

"Bones heal, pain is temporary, and chicks dig scars."
— Evil Knievel

HEAR YOUR STORY BOOKS

At **Hear Your Story**, we have created a line of books focused on giving each of us a place to tell the unique story of who we are, where we have been, and where we are going.

Sharing and hearing the stories of the people in our lives creates a closeness and understanding, ultimately strengthening our bonds.

Available at Amazon, all bookstores, and HearYourStoryBooks.com

- Mom, I Want to Hear Your Story: A Mother's Guided Journal to Share Her Life & Her Love

- Dad, I Want to Hear Your Story: A Father's Guided Journal to Share His Life & His Love

- Grandfather, I Want to Hear Your Story: A Grandfather's Guided Journal to Share His Life and His Love

- Tell Your Life Story: The Write Your Own Autobiography Guided Journal

- Life Gave Me You; I Want to Hear Your Story: A Guided Journal for Stepmothers to Share Their Life Story

- You Choose to Be My Dad; I Want to Hear Your Story: A Guided Journal for Stepdads to Share Their Life Story

HEAR YOUR STORY BOOKS

- To My Wonderful Aunt, I Want to Hear Your Story: A Guided Journal to Share Her Life and Her Love
- To My Uncle, I Want to Hear Your Story: A Guided Journal to Share His Life and His Love
- Mom, I Want to Learn Your Recipes: A Keepsake Memory Book to Gather and Preserve Your Favorite Family Recipes
- Dad, I Want to Learn Your Recipes: A Keepsake Memory Book to Gather and Preserve Your Favorite Family Recipes
- Grandmother, I Want to Learn Your Recipes: A Keepsake Memory Book to Gather and Preserve Your Favorite Family Recipes
- Grandfather, I Want to Learn Your Recipes: A Keepsake Memory Book to Gather and Preserve Your Favorite Family Recipes
- Aunt, I Want to Learn Your Recipes: A Keepsake Memory Book to Gather and Preserve Your Favorite Family Recipes
- Uncle, I Want to Learn Your Recipes: A Keepsake Memory Book to Gather and Preserve Your Favorite Family Recipes
- To My Girlfriend, I Want to Hear Your Story
- To My Boyfriend, I Want to Hear Your Story
- Mom & Me: Let's Learn Together Journal for Kids

DEDICATION

To Tommie Louis Mason
My Dad

You were my first example, my forever mentor.

We are alike in temperament
and the same in spirit.
The lesson of your life was
to live and love with all I am,
to never give up and to always find a way.

Most important of all,
you taught me to love who I am
and always believe that I deserve *amazing*.

Thank you for your love, your example, and your passion for the discovery of what is possible.

I Love You Dad.

Dear goodness, I miss you.

ABOUT THE AUTHOR

Jeffrey Mason is the creator and author of the best-selling **Hear Your Story®** line of books and is the founder of the company **Hear Your Story®**.

In response to his own father's fight with Alzheimer's, Jeffrey wrote his first two books, **Mom, I Want to Hear Your Story** and **Dad, I Want to Hear Your Story** in 2019. Since then, he has written and designed over 30 books, been published in four languages, and sold over 300,000 copies worldwide.

Jeffrey is dedicated to spreading the mission that the little things are the big things and that each of us has an incredible life story that needs to be shared and celebrated. He continues to create books that he hopes will guide people to reflect on and share their full life experience, while creating opportunities for talking, listening, learning, and understanding.

Hear Your Story® can be visited at **hearyourstorybooks.com** and Jeffrey can be contacted for questions, comments, podcasting, speaking engagements, or just a hello at **jeffrey.mason@hearyourstory.com**.

He would be grateful if you would help people find his books by leaving a review on Amazon. Your feedback helps him get better at this thing he loves.

To My Uncle, I Want to Hear Your Story

VIEW THIS BOOK ON YOUR COMPUTER

We invite you to also check out HearYourStory.com, where you can answer the questions in this book using your smart phone, tablet, or computer.

Answering the questions online at HearYourStory.com allows you to write as much as you want, to save your responses and revisit and revise them whenever you wish, and to print as many copies as you need for you and your whole family.

Please note there is a small one-time charge to cover the cost of maintaining the site.

Copyright © 2023 EYP Publishing, LLC, Hear Your Story Books, & Jeffrey Mason

All rights reserved. No part of this publication may be reproduced, distributed, or transmitted in any form or by any means, including photocopying, recording, computer, or other electronic or mechanical methods, without the prior written permission of the publisher, except in the case of brief quotations embodied in critical reviews and certain other noncommercial uses permitted by copyright law. For permission requests, write to the publisher, addressed "Attention: Permissions Coordinator," to customerservice@eyppublishing.com.

ISBN: 978-1-955034-03-6

Made in the USA
Las Vegas, NV
09 June 2024

90924440R00066